Pet Goldfish

Julia Barnes

GARETH**STEVENS**
GS
P U B L I S H I N G
A Member of the WRC Media Family of Companies

Please visit our web site at: **www.garethstevens.com**
For a free color catalog describing Gareth Stevens Publishing's
list of high-quality books and multimedia programs, call
1-800-542-2595 (USA) or 1-800-387-3178 (Canada).
Gareth Stevens Publishing's fax: (414) 332-3567.

Library of Congress Cataloging-in-Publication Data

Barnes, Julia, 1955-
   Pet goldfish / Julia Barnes. — North American ed.
    p. cm. — (Pet pals)
   Includes bibliographical references and index.
   ISBN-10: 0-8368-6778-5 – ISBN-13: 978-0-8368-6778-7 (lib. bdg.)
   1. Goldfish—Juvenile literature. I. Title.
SF458.G6B365   2007
639.3'7484—dc22   2006042376

This edition first published in 2007 by
Gareth Stevens Publishing
A Member of the WRC Media Family of Companies
330 West Olive Street, Suite 100
Milwaukee, Wisconsin 53212 USA

This U.S. edition copyright © 2007 by Gareth Stevens, Inc.
Original edition copyright © 2006 by Westline Publishing,
P.O. Box 8, Lydney, Gloucestershire, GL15 6YD, United Kingdom.

Gareth Stevens series editor: Leifa Butrick
Gareth Stevens cover design: Dave Kowalski
Gareth Stevens art direction: Tammy West

Picture Credits:
All images copyright © 2006 by Westline Publishing.

Printed in the United States of America

1 2 3 4 5 6 7 8 9 10 09 08 07 06

Cover: Three goldfish swim in a tank.

Contents

Words that appear in the glossary are printed in **boldface**
type the first time the word occurs in the text.

The First Goldfish

The Chinese caught fish from the wild for food about 4,500 years ago.

More than four thousand years ago, the crucian carp, a small brown fish, was a common sight in the cool, slow-moving, freshwater rivers and streams of southern China. The Chinese caught carp from the wild and then set up their own farms to breed carp and sell them for food. Fish farmers noticed that some carp were brighter colors than others — more orange than brown — and they decided to breed these fish to produce gold-colored fish.

By the time of the Chinese Sung Dynasty, about one thousand years ago, the goldfish was a recognized breed. Goldfish, however, were no longer raised as food. Instead, they swam among the water lilies in beautiful ponds. Keeping fish as pets became a popular hobby among the Chinese.

Fancy Goldfish

The Japanese also caught carp from the wild, and they developed their own breed of pet fish, called koi. Koi are much bigger than goldfish and come in a dazzling array of colors. Today, koi are highly prized

An ornamental fish pond was a sign of wealth in both China and Japan.

These symbols are the word *goldfish* written in Chinese characters.

all over the world. The rare **varieties** cost hundreds of thousands of dollars.

In the fourteenth century, the Japanese turned their fish-breeding skills to goldfish, and they developed spectacular new varieties. The Japanese kept their fancy goldfish in ponds that were decorated with plants and sculptures. Wooden bridges and stepping-stone pathways gave people a good view of the fish.

Spreading Worldwide

In the nineteenth century, news of fancy goldfish spread outside China and Japan. Ships from the East sailed to Europe, carrying silks, spices, and interesting plants and animals, including fancy goldfish.

Europeans were fascinated by the fish from the East, and they began keeping fish as well. The first goldfish exported to North America, in 1878, created a huge demand for the fish. Goldfish were soon the most popular pet fish in the world.

Skilled breeders have developed many colors and varieties of goldfish.

Perfect Pets

Hundreds of different fish breeds live in aquariums, but goldfish are a long-time favorite.

oldfish make perfect pets for many reasons.

- Goldfish are beautiful to look at.
- Goldfish are inexpensive.
- The many different varieties of goldfish offer a wide choice.
- Goldfish do not take up very much room.
- Goldfish can be kept indoors in an aquarium or outdoors in a pond in **temperate climates**.

- Goldfish are hardy fish and can live up to twenty-five years. Fancy varieties live about fourteen years.

Golden Rule

Keeping goldfish is a perfect solution for people who suffer from **pet allergies** and cannot have animals with fur in their homes.

Bristol shubunkin, moor, and oranda varieties of goldfish can live together in the same tank.

A goldfish can live a long, healthy life if it is kept in proper conditions.

Good Luck

Keeping fish can have a calming effect on people. The Chinese system of *feng shui*, which helps people live in harmony with their surroundings, puts a high value on goldfish and calls them baby dragons. The Chinese word for fish is *yu*, which is the same as the word for success, so keeping goldfish in a home or an office is considered good luck.

Goldfish Needs

Goldfish are easy to keep, but, like all living creatures, goldfish still have certain needs.

- Goldfish need food every day.
- Goldfish need fresh water that is free of harmful chemicals.
- Goldfish need a tank that is the right size for the number of fish in it.

- Goldfish need someone to watch over their health.
- Goldfish need their aquariums cleaned regularly.
- Goldfish need someone to take care of them when their owners are away for more than a day.

Record Breaker

The oldest known goldfish was named Tish and lived to be forty-three years old.

Goldfish Homes

Unlike tropical fish, goldfish are **cold water fish**, which means they can live in cold water without special heating equipment. Some hardy varieties of goldfish live in outdoor ponds all year round and survive cold temperatures.

A Goldfish's Body

Each part of a goldfish's body suits its main activity — swimming.

Inner Ear
A goldfish's ears are inside its body. Goldfish do not like loud noises and will dart away to find safe hiding places.

Brain
Goldfish used to be thought of as the dimwits of the animal kingdom, with memories lasting only three seconds. Now, evidence shows that a goldfish recognizes members of its own **school** and knows when it is feeding time.

Nostrils
Goldfish use their sense of smell to find food. They can also smell chemicals in their water.

Eyes
A goldfish's eyes bulge out slightly, giving the goldfish good all-around vision, even though it cannot turn its head. Compared to many species of fish, goldfish have excellent vision and can see objects 15 feet (4.5 meters) away.

Gills
Goldfish do not have lungs for breathing. They use their gills to take in oxygen from the water and to get rid of carbon dioxide.

Dorsal Fin

Dorsal fins help goldfish balance in the water. Some fancy varieties do not have dorsal fins, which makes them poor swimmers.

Lateral Line

A goldfish has a set of nerves in a line along its body that alerts the goldfish to any disturbances in the water.

Golden Rule

A goldfish is **cold-blooded**, which means that its body temperature changes with the temperature of the water. Goldfish can withstand a wide range of temperatures but not sudden temperature changes.

Color

The traditional metallic color of a goldfish comes from a reflective material beneath the fish's scales.

Caudal Fin

The caudal fin, or tail fin, propels a goldfish through water. In fancy varieties of goldfish, the tail fin is split down the middle forming twin tails.

Scales

Bony scales that overlap each other cover a goldfish from its head to its tail, **streamlining** its body so the goldfish can swim easily.

Pectoral Fin

The fins on each side of its body help a goldfish steer.

Anal Fin

The anal fins near the back of a goldfish's body also help the fish balance in the water.

Vent

A goldfish gets rid of waste through its vent.

Goldfish Varieties

Take your pick from more than one hundred varieties of goldfish.

Goldfish come in many different sizes, shapes, and colors, and some are much easier to take care of than others. If you choose the more unusual varieties, you will have to take care to meet their special needs.

• Fancy goldfish, which include all the twin-tailed varieties, must be kept in aquariums. They cannot survive in outdoor ponds. They need water temperatures between 74 and 78 °Fahrenheit

(23 and 25 °Celsius). Hardy goldfish can live in temperatures between 50 and 76 °F (10 and 24 °C).

• Some fancy varieties have very delicate fins. Because their fins rip easily, it is important not to have jagged objects in their tanks.

• Twin-tailed goldfish and varieties without dorsal fins cannot swim as well as the single-tailed varieties. These slower fish will lose out if they have to compete with single-tailed fish for food.

Common goldfish

London Shubunkin

Single-tailed Goldfish
These goldfish are tough and grow to be about 4 inches (10 centimeters) long or even longer.

Common Goldfish
Traditional goldfish can be any color from golden red to pale yellow. They are an ideal choice for new fish keepers. These fish can live in aquariums or ponds.

Shubunkin
Some shubunkins are beautifully colored fish with blue-silver bodies with patches of black, red, brown, yellow, and violet. The London shubunkin, however, looks more like the common goldfish and can live in an aquarium or a pond. The Bristol shubunkin has larger fins and a fancy tail. It needs an aquarium.

Fantail
As its name suggests, the fantail goldfish has a fan-shaped tail. It also has a short, round body.

Comet
An all-American breed, the comet has a single tail fin that is sometimes as long as its body. A comet can swim very fast over short distances. It is usually yellow, but some comets have white bodies with bright red coloring along their backs. Comets are suitable for either aquariums or ponds.

Fantail

Moor

Fancy Goldfish

Fancy varieties of goldfish do well only if they are kept in aquariums. Fancy goldfish are smaller than single-tailed goldfish. They are also more expensive and may have more health problems.

Veiltail

The tail fin of a veiltail hangs in folds, its anal fin is long, and its dorsal fin is very tall. Veiltails are slow swimmers, and sharp objects can cut their flowing fins.

Moor

This goldfish is jet-black. It has the same shape as a veiltail and is just as delicate. A moor's eyes stick out a long way, which is why this fish is often called the telescope-eyed moor.

Lionhead

A lionhead is a very poor swimmer because it has no dorsal fin. It has an egg-shaped body and a growth on its head that looks like a raspberry. The growth is called a hood.

Lionhead

Ryunkin

A ryunkin has a short body, a steeply curved back, and flowing fins. It is round in shape and looks like a butterfly from behind. It is the easiest of the fancy goldfish to keep.

Oranda

The oranda is similar in shape to the lionhead. It also has a growth on its head, but the oranda has a dorsal fin. Most Orandas are white with red heads. They are known as "gooseheads" in the United States.

Oranda

Bubble Eye

This goldfish is easy to recognize. It has large sacs that look like bubbles under its eyes. The Bubble Eye is a poor swimmer, and its bubbles are easily damaged.

Bubble Eye

Pompom

The pompom is named after the two "cheerleader" pompoms above its nostrils.

Pompom

The Aquarium

Most first-time fish keepers prefer to keep their goldfish in aquariums.

Goldfish need to have enough room to swim around without feeling crowded. Their water also needs enough oxygen in it for the fish to remain healthy. A rectangular-shaped tank, measuring a minimum of 2 feet (60 cm) long, 1 foot (30 cm) wide, and 1 foot (30 cm) deep is fine, but bigger tanks are even better.

Finding a Place for a Tank

A fish tank full of water is very heavy. It must stand on a sturdy shelf or table. A tank also needs to be near an electric outlet. While deciding where to put your aquarium, consider the following:

• A living room or a family room is a great place for an aquarium because people

When you buy a tank, ask a specialist at the store about the right number of fish to keep in a tank of that size.

Goldfish like to have company, but they do not like to be crowded.

usually have the most chances to enjoy the fish there. Just make sure your goldfish do not get too much attention from family members or from visitors who may tap on the glass and upset the fish.

- A kitchen is not a good place for a tank because cooking and cleaning fumes can be harmful to fish.
- A bathroom is not good for fish because the temperature changes too much.
- Do not put an aquarium close to a radiator or a heat vent because the heat might affect the water temperature.

- An aquarium should not be in direct sunlight for more than four hours a day, or it will be overrun with **algae**, a green plant that grows on the inside of a tank's glass walls.

How Many Fish?

In the wild, small fish swim in schools to make it harder for **predators** to attack them. Although a single goldfish may be safe in your aquarium, it will not be happy because it will feel as if it is always exposed to danger. You should keep more than one goldfish, but be careful not to keep too many. Too many fish will make the water very dirty.

A filter can be hidden under gravel in a tank and still keep the water clean.

Keeping the Tank Clean

Like all living creatures, goldfish produce waste. An aquarium needs a filter so the fish will have clean water to swim in. A filter breaks down the waste that builds up in the water.

Several different types of filters are available. A mechanical filter collects the dirt in a tank. It can attach to the side of a tank, or it can be placed underneath the gravel at the bottom of a tank. A mechanical filter needs to be cleaned every two weeks by rinsing it under the faucet.

Bright Lights

Fish do not need lights in an aquarium, but lights look good, particularly in the evening.

Some types of filters attach to the side of an aquarium.

Many tanks come with hoods that have fluorescent light bulbs in them. Do not leave the lights on for a long time, however, especially if no one is in the room to enjoy them. Light encourages algae growth, and the glass walls of the aquarium will quickly begin to look dull and cloudy.

Cat-Safe

If you have a cat, make sure you buy a cover or hood for your tank, or your cat may try its paw at fishing. Even if the cat does not succeed in catching a fish, a paw dipped in the water would frighten your goldfish. The cat might also knock over objects in the tank.

A curious kitten cannot resist watching fish, so buying a cover for an aquarium might be a good idea.

Tank Setup

Create an aquarium **environment** that looks good and is safe for your goldfish.

Start at the Bottom

The bottom of an aquarium should be covered with gravel. Use either colored or natural looking stones. Wash the gravel before you put it into the tank, and then form a gravel slope from the back of the tank to the front. If you put a filter under the gravel, cover the filter with 3 to 4 inches (7 to 10 cm) of gravel.

Decorate

Be creative and have some fun when you choose ornaments for your tank. You may like fairy-tale castles and deep-sea divers, or you may prefer rocks and natural wood. Goldfish seem to like rocks with holes or caves in them that they can swim through. Before buying tank decorations, ask the staff at the pet store if the items are suitable for a goldfish aquarium. If you plan to keep fancy goldfish, you do not want to buy rocks or ornaments with sharp edges that could damage delicate fins.

Goldfish like rocks and ornaments they can swim through and hide in.

Canadian pondweed

Golden Rule

Put plants in your aquarium when the tank is half full of water so you can place them where you want without getting soaked!

Plants

Goldfish are plant nibblers. Some fish keepers use plastic plants that will not need replacing, but aquariums look more attractive with living plants. Goldfish enjoy hiding among the plants as well as eating them for occasional snacks! The following plants grow well in cold water tanks:

Water milfoil

Java fern

- Canadian pondweed (*Anacharis densa*) — The long stems of this plant have dark green leaves. The stems can be cut to the right lengths for your tank.
- Water milfoil (*Myriolphyllum*) — Goldfish like this hardy plant because they can hide behind its leaves.
- Java fern (*Microsorium*) — This broad-leaved plant grows out of a thick root.

Make sure that plants are secure in the gravel so the plants cannot easily be uprooted.

Adding Water

You might think that you can just turn on the kitchen tap and fill your tank with water, but it is not quite that simple. A healthy aquarium needs high-quality water. Tap water is not suitable for fish for a number of reasons:

- Tap water may contain chemicals, such as **chlorine**, that are harmful to fish.
- Tap water may contain high levels of nitrates and phosphates that encourage algae growth.
- Tiny living creatures that could harm your fish may be living in your tap water.

To solve these problems, you can use a chemical dechlorinator that prepares tap water for use in an aquarium. Dechlorinators are available at most pet stores. When you are ready to fill your tank with water, ask an experienced fish keeper to help you figure out how much dechlorinator to add to the water.

Water Temperature

Do not use hot water from the tap to fill a fish tank because hot water often contains copper, which is harmful to fish. Cold water will gradually reach room temperature and be comfortable for most varieties of goldfish.

After the tank is set up, turn on the filter to prepare the water for the fish.

Be Patient

Do not rush off to buy your goldfish as soon as you have filled the tank! Wait a week before putting fish into it. In a week, the water will have warmed up and the filter will have created the correct **chemical balance** in the water. A simple test kit, available from pet stores, can help you check the water. You could also ask an expert to help you test the water, after you have set up an aquarium, to see if it is all right for fish.

Fish swim comfortably in dechlorinated water.

The Right Choice

Look for the signs of a healthy goldfish.

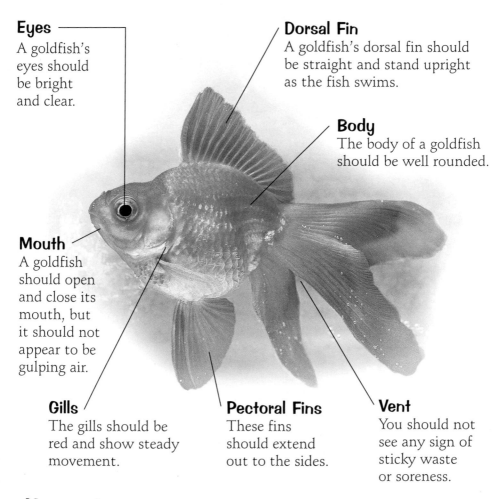

Eyes
A goldfish's eyes should be bright and clear.

Dorsal Fin
A goldfish's dorsal fin should be straight and stand upright as the fish swims.

Body
The body of a goldfish should be well rounded.

Mouth
A goldfish should open and close its mouth, but it should not appear to be gulping air.

Gills
The gills should be red and show steady movement.

Pectoral Fins
These fins should extend out to the sides.

Vent
You should not see any sign of sticky waste or soreness.

Movement
A goldfish should swim smoothly. A fish that wobbles, tilts, or rests on the bottom might be sick.

Scales
A goldfish's scales should be free of spots, bumps, and woolly patches.

Color
The goldfish's color should be dense and even.

These goldfish look crowded in the plastic bag, but it is better to keep them in a bag until the water is ready for them.

When buying a goldfish, go to a store that specializes in aquarium fish and equipment. The staff there should be experienced fish keepers who can give you valuable advice.

Look around the store to see if the tanks are clean and well cared for. The water in the tanks should be clear, and the fish should not be crowded. Different varieties of goldfish should be kept in separate tanks, and there should be no sign of sick fish.

Arriving Home

The goldfish you choose will be put in a plastic bag full of water for the journey home. Do not pour your fish straight into the tank the minute you arrive home. Goldfish do not like shocks, such as sudden changes in temperature. Wait until the water in the plastic bag is the same temperature as the water in the tank.

- Open the top of the bag, and let the bag float in the tank with the fish in it.
- After twenty minutes, let some tank water pour into the bag. Then release the fish.

Golden Rule

When you start a new tank, buy a couple of fish and let them get used to the aquarium for a week or two before adding more fish to the tank.

Feeding Goldfish

Fish in the wild find their own food, but aquarium fish rely on their owners for a healthy diet.

Goldfish are hardy fish. They are not too fussy about the foods they eat, but they still need **vitamins** and **carbohydrates** to help them grow and to fight diseases. They also need a small amount of **protein** to build muscle. Fortunately, goldfish keepers do not have to worry about preparing food that has all the right **nutrients**. Good fish food comes ready-made.

Dried Food

Goldfish food comes in dried forms — as flakes, granules, or pellets. Many different brands are available, but read the labels to be sure you are buying food that is specially made for goldfish.

Supplements

Wild goldfish and pond goldfish will eat a lot of weeds and other plants that are not available to aquarium fish. To give your goldfish plant food (and to save your aquarium plants), you can drop a slice of cucumber into the tank or hang some freshly washed lettuce inside the tank.

Sprinkle dried food on the surface of the water, and your fish will quickly come to feed.

You must learn how much food to give your goldfish so they stay fit and healthy.

Live Food

Goldfish that live in ponds eat shrimp, worms, and snails. Aquarium fish will certainly enjoy live food as an occasional treat, too. The easiest way to supply live food is to buy some daphnia, or water fleas, at a pet store. Make sure you buy a small quantity so your goldfish eat them all in one feeding.

Overfeeding

Be sure you do not make the mistake of overfeeding your goldfish. Goldfish are always eager to come to the surface when you offer food, so do not feed them more than twice a day. Too much food is very bad for goldfish. They could develop health problems if they eat too much. Also, leftover food will rot in the water and **pollute** it, which could kill the fish.

Vacations

If you will be away from home for more than a day, ask someone to look after your aquarium. You can buy slow-releasing food that will last for a few days, but, ideally, someone should keep an eye on your fish while you are away.

Golden Rule

Feed your goldfish twice a day. Give them only as much food as they can eat within five to ten minutes. A floating feeding ring keeps food in one place so your fish can find it easily.

Goldfish Care

Keep a close watch on your aquarium so you can spot signs of trouble early.

When you feed your goldfish, take a few minutes to study the fish to be sure they all appear healthy. Be sure the tank's filter is operating and that the plants have not been uprooted.

Testing the Water

Test the water every week to make sure it is suitable for your goldfish. You can use the same test kit you used when you first set up your aquarium. Ask an experienced fish keeper to help you the first time.

Water Changes

If a water test shows a poor balance of chemicals, you need to change the water in the tank. Generally, fish keepers do a **partial water change** every two weeks to keep a tank clean and healthy. Removing 10 to 20 percent of the water at a time is much easier than making a complete change.

A healthy goldfish will swim smoothly through the water and will quickly come to the surface at feeding time.

If you do not change the water in your tank, it will become polluted, and your goldfish will suffer.

- First, fill a bucket with cold water and place it by the tank. Wait a couple of hours for the fresh water to reach room temperature.
- To remove water from the tank, use a plastic tube about 0.5 inches (12 millimeters) in diameter and 4 to 5 feet (1.25 to 1.5 m) long.
- Put the plastic tube into the tank and fill it with water. When the tube is full, place a finger over both ends so the water does not run out.

- Drop one end of the tube to the bottom of the tank and put the other in an empty bucket on the floor, at a level lower than the tank.
- When you release your fingers, the water will begin to flow from the tank to the bucket.
- Take the tube out of the tank when you have removed enough water.
- You can now add the fresh water to the tank.

Algae Growth

Algae are small green plants that grow in water and can quickly cover the sides of a tank. Sunlight and electric lights help algae grow. Although algae are not harmful to goldfish, they spoil the look of the aquarium. Algae can be removed quite easily by using an algae scraper once a week.

Golden Rule

Remember to add dechlorinator to the fresh water before you pour the water into the tank.

27

Goldfish Behavior

Watch for signs that tell you how your goldfish are feeling.

Happy Goldfish

A contented goldfish will be active, swimming with ease among the plants and rocks and coming to the surface to feed. Its fins will flow freely, and the fish will appear bright and alert.

Stressed Goldfish

Fish are very sensitive, and they will show signs of **stress** if their environment is not to their liking. A fish, for example, may feel that the tank is crowded. Other fish may be bullying the fish, or there may be too few plants in the tank so the fish has no hiding places. Signs of stress in a fish include:

- swimming with its fins held tight to its body
- hanging in corners with its head down or up
- looking nervous, as if it were trying to escape

This fish is happy and healthy. It is swimming freely and is interested in its surroundings.

When one goldfish bullies another fish in the tank, the bullied fish is likely to show signs of stress.

- showing no interest in food
- appearing lighter or darker in color than usual

If you see any of these signs, check your aquarium carefully and try to figure out why the fish may be stressed. Then make changes to provide a better environment.

Sleeping Goldfish

Because goldfish have no eyelids, they cannot close their eyes when they sleep. A sleeping goldfish will sink to a low position in the water, usually somewhere out of sight, and will turn a paler color.

Greetings

You cannot train a goldfish to shake hands, but your fish will recognize you when you approach the tank. They will rise to the surface and swim rapidly back and forth, which is their way of saying hello!

Fish Signal

You may see your goldfish tip up, with its head resting on the bottom of the tank and its tail held high. The goldfish has found some food, and its tail is a signal to other goldfish to swim over and enjoy the feast.

Glossary

algae: tiny green plants that grow in water

carbohydrates: foods containing sugars and starches

chemical balance: the right mixture of chemicals that makes the water suitable for fish to live in

chlorine: a chemical in tap water that is harmful to fish

cold-blooded: describing a living thing whose body temperature changes with its surroundings

cold water fish: types of fish that can live in cold water, as opposed to tropical fish, which need warm water

environment: the conditions or surroundings in which something lives

nutrients: nourishing substances in food

partial water change: replacing part of the water in a tank

pet allergies: reactions to living with furry animals, such as breathing difficulties, skin disorders, and watery eyes

pollute: to make something impure or unclean

predators: living things that kill and eat other living things

protein: complex food found in meat, milk, and eggs

school: a group of fish that swim together

streamlining: producing a smooth shape

stress: a condition caused by anger or fear

temperate climates: moderate climates that do not produce very hot or very cold weather

varieties: different types

vitamins: substances present in food, and needed for certain bodily functions

More Books to Read

101 Facts About Goldfish
Julia Barnes
(Gareth Stevens)

A Pet's Life: Goldfish
Anita Ganeri
(Heinemann Library)

All About Your Goldfish
Bradley Viner
(Barron's Educational)

Goldfish
Looking After My Pet (series)
David Alderton
(Lorenz Books)

Web Sites

There's Something Fishy Going On!
www.FisHedz.com/

Ben's Fish Web Site
www.bensfish.wanadoo.co.uk/coldwaterfish.htm

Glimmering Goldfish
www.goldfishinfo.com

Pet Station Fish Station: Goldfish Varietites
www.petstation.com/goldfish-varieties.html

Koko's Goldfish World
www.kokosgoldfish.com

Publisher's note to educators and parents: Our editors have carefully reviewed these Web sites to ensure that they are suitable for children. Many Web sites change frequently, however, and we cannot guarantee that a site's future contents will continue to meet our high standards of quality and educational value. Be advised that children should be closely supervised whenever they access the Internet.

Index